STO

D0880949

EASY
CRAFT
SERIES

what to make with pine cones

By Geneviève Ploquin
Photographs by Boris Téplitzky

CONTENTS

 STERLING PUBLISHING CO., INC.   **NEW YORK**

Oak Tree Press Co., Ltd.   London & Sydney

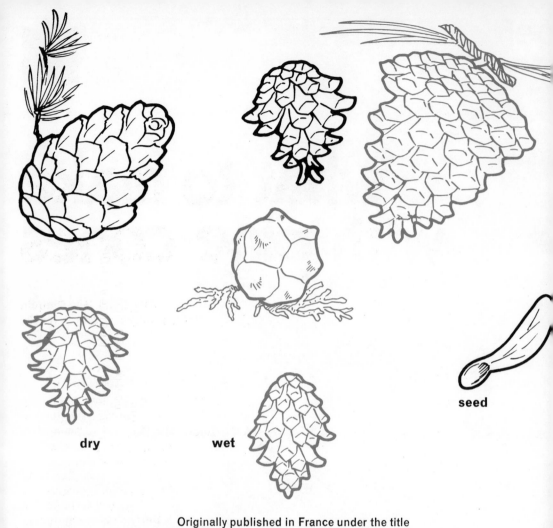

dry

wet

seed

Originally published in France under the title
"Avec des Pommes de Pin" © 1975 by Editions Fleurus, Paris.
Translated by Maxine Hobson.
Copyright © 1976 by Sterling Publishing Co., Inc.
419 Park Avenue South, New York, N.Y. 10016
Distributed in Australia and New Zealand by Oak Tree Press Co., Ltd.,
P.O. Box J34, Brickfield Hill, Sydney 2000, N.S.W.
Distributed in the United Kingdom and elsewhere in the British Commonwealth
by Ward Lock Ltd., 116 Baker Street, London W1
Manufactured in the United States of America
All rights reserved
Library of Congress Catalog Card No.: 76–19823

Sterling ISBN 0-8069-5412-4 Trade   Oak Tree 7061- 2530–4
5413-2 Library

 is a registered trademark of Editions Fleurus, Paris.

before you begin...

Pine cones are the fruits of various conifers or evergreens. The projects in this book show mainly the cones of the ordinary pine trees growing in the woods, but parasol pines, firs, Norway spruce, and yews all have differently shaped cones with woody scales.

You can gather pine cones in any season. Look for them on the carpet of dried needles under the trees.

Pine cones are different colors according to their age. Young, they are light brown, the tips of the scales yellowish; when you varnish them the body of the scales turns a beautiful purplish red. Older, they darken and turn grey; the tips of the scales are pale grey, sometimes greenish when rain has dampened them a lot.

Don't limit yourself only to the most beautiful cones; use large, medium, and even some very tiny ones. Also, gather some old ones because their scales are easily removed.

After collecting cones you must clean them with a large paintbrush or paint scrubber; sometimes it is even necessary to wash them. Use a fine feather to remove the little pieces that hide under each scale.

Don't be surprised to see the cones opening or closing themselves; it is one of their strange habits. When the humidity is high, such as when it rains, the scales bend themselves towards the center, almost closing completely. On the other hand, dryness makes them open up. Once varnished, however, they no longer are affected by humidity.

MATERIALS

To make things with pine cones, you will need:

- a pen-knife
- wire cutter or heavy kitchen shears to remove the scales
- pliers for working with wire
- scissors, ruler, pencil, compass
- a large paintbrush for cleaning the cones
- paints
- wood glue
- some white glue, cardboard and paper

Any additional materials are listed with each project. Note that when you collect the pine cones, it is also easy to gather bunches of needles and some twigs from the branches, plus a few pebbles along the way. There are two other materials you may need:

- One is wood shavings, or pieces of wood veneer, which you can find at a woodworking shop or buy at a handicraft shop. They come in different sizes, colors and finishes.

- Modelling clay is another material you can use for your pine cone creations. You need the type that hardens by itself. You can then paint and varnish it. If you want to place pine cones on a base of modelling clay, you can add a drop of glue to hold them. When the instructions in a project say to use modelling clay, you can use plastic wood instead, because it is similar.

To make sure that the pine cones stick to each other or to other materials, use a two-step glueing method. First cover both parts with glue, let the glue dry a little, and add another drop of glue. Push the parts in place. Hold the two parts together by hand for several minutes. When the glue starts to set, lean the glued pieces against some books, small stones, or other type of support.

fir tree
PLAQUE

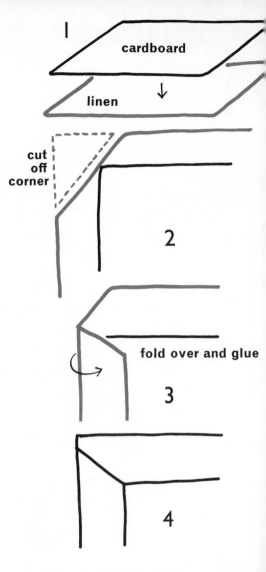

You can make a beautiful picture of anything you want using pine cones—try creating a house, a round tree, a castle, or whatever you wish. All you do is glue small, opened pine cones one next to the other.

For a background, you can use a big piece of white linen or other light-colored material such as burlap (hessian). Then the pretty color of the pine cone shows up well.

Here are the instructions for the tree in the color photograph.

MATERIALS

● a piece of stiff cardboard; cut it the size you want your picture to be

● a piece of linen or other material 2 inches (5 cm.) larger on all sides than the cardboard

● a pretty stone

● a small, straight twig or piece of rounded wood

● some pine cones, one smaller than the rest for the tip of the tree

● wood glue for the pine cones, fabric glue for the linen

● a picture hanger

CONSTRUCTION

● Place several lines of fabric glue on the cardboard. Turn the cardboard over and glue it to the middle of the linen or other material you chose (see drawing 1).

● Cut off the corners of the material as shown in drawing 2. Then glue the edges of the cloth to the cardboard, forming neat corners (see drawings 3 and 4).

● Clean and varnish the pine cones (see page 3 for how to do this). Varnish the stone.

● With the wood glue, glue the pine cones together in the shape of a tree. Then glue the whole tree to the background.

● Put the stone and the "trunk" in place and glue to the background.

● Glue a little hook on the back to hang your picture when it is finished.

a **SHEPHERD,** his **DOG,** & his **sheep**

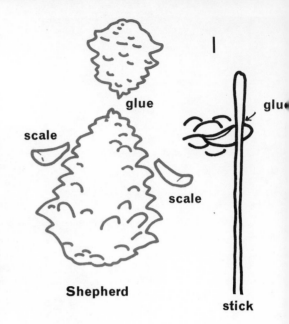

scale

glue

scale

Shepherd

I

glue

stick

Here is a brave shepherd with his faithful dog who guards the sheep. You can make as large a flock of sheep as you want.

THE SHEPHERD

MATERIALS

● a pine cone large enough for the shepherd's body and cloak and a smaller one for his head
● 2 large scales (try to pick ones the same color as the pine cones)
● a very straight stick for the staff
● glue

CONSTRUCTION

Drawing 1 shows you how to make the shepherd.
● Stand the pine cone "body" on its base. If the pine cone doesn't stand up on its base very well, use some modelling clay to hold it.
● Glue the head on upside down. It helps if you can overlap the scales of the body and the head.
● Glue one scale on each side of the body to make the hands stick out of the cloak.
● Glue the shepherd's staff to one of his hands.

● Make a pipe for the shepherd from a very tiny twig. Glue a small piece of a scale to the end of it.

THE SHEEP

MATERIALS

For each sheep you need:
● 2 small pine cones, one for the body and one for the head
● 5 burnt wooden matches (or 5 small twigs)

CONSTRUCTION

Drawing 2 shows you how to make each sheep.
● Carve the ends of 4 matches into points. Cover them with glue. Put the matches in place between the scales to make the legs. Place the two front legs fairly far apart and slant them towards the front so the sheep can stand up well.
● Carve the two ends of the last match (for the "neck") into points. Stick the neck into the head and the body between scales. Add a drop of glue.

6

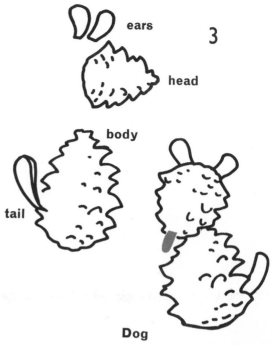

ears

3

head

body

tail

Dog

matches

Sheep

body

neck

front

side

2

THE DOG

MATERIALS

- 2 medium pine cones for the head and body
- 3 scales: 2 little ones for ears, 1 larger one for the tail
- a tiny piece of red felt
- glue

CONSTRUCTION

Drawing 3 shows how to make the dog.

- Place the pine cone forming the body on its base. Slant it forward a little. You can use some modelling clay to hold the base in place.
- Glue the head in place.
- Put glue on the tip of the "tail" scale and put it between 2 scales. Do the same thing for the ears.
- Glue on a red felt tongue.

7

a fish, a WADING BIRD, and an owl

You'll have fun making the three little pine cone animals described here, and you will want to think of other animals to create.

THE FISH

MATERIALS

- a pretty, fairly long pine cone
- 2 small stones and one longer stone
- 3 bunches of green pine needles
- glue, varnish

CONSTRUCTION

- Glue the longest bunch of needles to the tip of the pine cone for the tail.
- Glue 2 other bunches of needles to each side of the pine cone for the fins.
- Glue on the stone to make the eyes and the mouth.
- Varnish everything but the needles.

LONG-LEGGED BIRD

Here's how to make an easy long-legged bird. It can be as large or small as you want, because it's not a real bird! You can decorate it with real feathers or with bunches of green or dry pine needles.

MATERIALS

- a large pine cone for the body and a small one for the head
- a little wire for the legs that is strong enough to hold up the large pine cone body
- a twig (try to find a curved one) for the neck and a thinner one for the beak
- some feathers or bunches of pine needles
- pliers to shape the wire
- glue, varnish

CONSTRUCTION

- Curve the wire to form a foot. Then make a U-shape as high as you want the legs to be. Then make the other foot (see drawing 1).
- Place this wire in the pine cone between the scales. Push it down to make it tight so the feet will stay in place (see drawing 2).
- Carve the two ends of the twig into a point to make the neck. Push the neck in-between 2 scales in the head. If it doesn't stay in place, put some glue on the end of the twig.

● Put glue on the other end and stick it into the body, also between 2 scales.

● Carve the ends of the twig for the beak into points. Then glue the beak in place.

Put some pine needles between 2 scales on the top of the head.

Glue a bunch of pine needles between 2 scales for the tail. Then glue on 2 bunches to make the wings (see drawing 3).

Varnish the head and the body.

put wire around pine cone

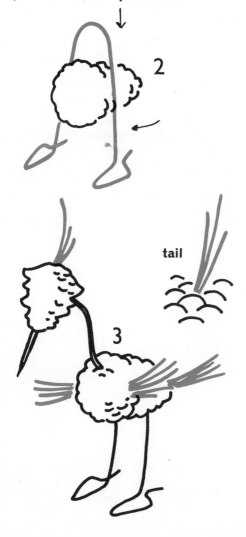

2

tail

3

make a U-shape bend

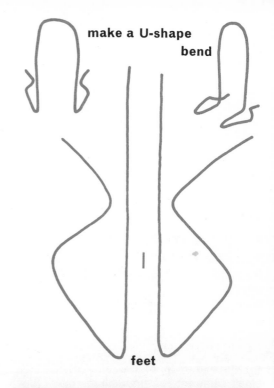

feet

9

THE OWL

It's really easy to make owls from pine cones of all sizes! Why not make a collection?

MATERIALS

- a well opened pine cone
- 4 large scales
- some yellow and black construction paper
- some modelling clay
- glue, varnish

CONSTRUCTION

- Place the tip of the pine cone on a small amount of modelling clay (see drawing 4). Be sure the pine cone is straight.
- Choose the best side of the pine cone for the owl's face. Then stick 2 scales into the clay to make the feet (see drawing 5).
- With a pen-knife, carefully separate the top scales. Place 2 scales to form the discs that all owls have here (see drawing 6). (These discs are sometimes called ears, but they aren't.)
- Follow drawing 7 to cut out 2 yellow eyes and 2 black pupils from construction paper. Use a few drops of glue to place the eyes on the edges of the scales.
- Let the modelling clay dry well.
- Varnish everything but the paper.

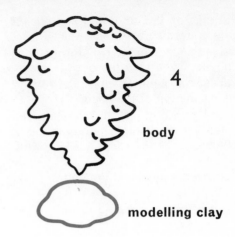

4 body

modelling clay

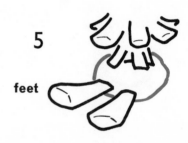

5 feet

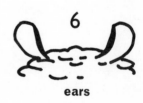

6 ears

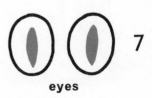

7 eyes

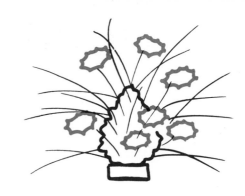

Here's a great way to make a light and natural arrangement of dried flowers. Use a pine cone base. For the arrangement itself, you can use grasses and flowers you gathered yourself or else dried flowers you can buy from a florist or in a crafts and hobby shop.

MATERIALS

● a large, well opened pine cone with a nice shape

● some dried plants such as grasses, herbs, wild oats, or whatever else you can find

● several dried flowers

● a small base made of wood, cork, or even a little piece of modelling clay; the important thing is for the pine cone to stand up straight

● glue, varnish

CONSTRUCTION

● Varnish the pine cone. Let it dry.

● Glue the pine cone to the base you chose.

● Now make the arrangement: Begin by placing the important parts, say the dried flowers, together so that you like the way they look. If the flowers have wire stems, wind the wire around the pine cone. Cut the wire and then push the ends into the pine cone. If the flower doesn't have a wire stem, just glue the stem to the pine cone scales. If the stem touches a few scales, add a drop of glue to all of them. Then fill in the arrangement with the other dried plants. Don't add too many or your arrangement will look sloppy. To finish, put in some tall grasses to give "lift" to the bouquet.

a **BISON**

• Cut the wood shavings in strips about ½ inch (7 or 8 mm.) long. Curl them with some scissors in the direction of the grain (see drawing 3). Glue in place following the color photograph.

• Glue the legs the same as you glued the head. Each base of a small leg cone should touch the edges of 3 scales on the body so the bison stands up straight (see drawing 4).

The color and shape of pine cones are just right for making this wild animal—a bison.

MATERIALS

• a large, long pine cone for the body, a medium-sized one for the head, and 4 small ones to make the legs

• some wood shavings or wood veneer (or else some narrow strips of beige construction paper)

• 2 small pieces of twigs cut to the shape of horns

• glue, varnish, brush for the varnish

CONSTRUCTION

• Varnish the 6 pine cones.

• When the pine cones are completely dry, attach the head to the body. Put some glue on the base of the head and stick it in place. Then take the head out and let the glue dry almost completely. Then add another drop of glue, put the head in place again and let it dry. It helps to prop up the two parts so they dry in the right place (see drawing 1).

• Glue the horns in place between the scales (see drawing 2) (the color photograph shows you where). If you can't find a small twig to cut for the horns, you can stick some modelling clay around a small piece of wire curved to the horns' shape. Paint the clay to look like horns.

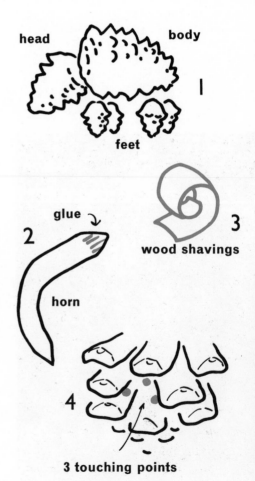

head   body

I

feet

glue

2

horn

3

wood shavings

4

3 touching points

SUN and RAIN indicator

A real rain and sun indicator is called a hygrometer. This is a special instrument used to measure humidity. You can easily make one using a pine cone because one special feature of pine cones is that they tell how much humidity the air has by opening or closing. Even if your home-made hygrometer doesn't tell you ahead of time what the weather will be, at least you can have fun seeing it work.

The opening and closing of the pine cone's scales are very important. You can see this clearly if you glue a twig that moves to mark the weather on a special background under one of the scales (the color photograph shows how this looks).

Place your hygrometer out-of-doors in a spot where it won't be rained on. If you leave it inside the house, it won't be able to tell the right weather because the heat and indoor air will affect the pine cone.

MATERIALS

● a pine cone that is young and in good condition
● a slightly curved twig
● some very strong cardboard for the base
● soft-tipped markers
● a little wire, a fine pick, awl or other sharp tool, pliers
● glue
● picture hook

CONSTRUCTION

● Glue the picture hook to the back of the cardboard.
● Place the pine cone on the cardboard base. Mark the spot where the wire will go between the scales (drawing 1 shows where).
● Cut two pieces of wire.
● Make 4 holes in the cardboard with a fine pick or other sharp tool.

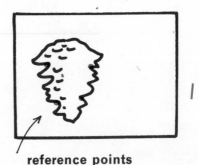

reference points

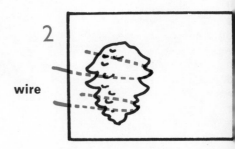

wire

14

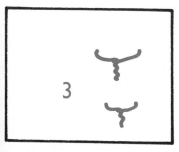

3

back of the cardboard

sunny

clear

overcast

cloudy

rain

5

scales

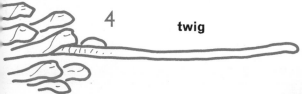

4

twig

● Push one end of a piece of wire from the back through the cardboard. Stretch the wire across the top of the pine cone and then put the end back through the cardboard (see drawing 2).

● With pliers, twist the two ends of the wire together on the back of the cardboard to fasten them (don't twist them too tightly) (see drawing 3).

● Do the same with a wire at the bottom of the pine cone.

● Glue the twig under a scale (see drawing 4).

● Now decorate the background with the different types of weather. To mark the weather (such as rain or sun) correctly, hang your hygrometer outside for a few days and watch what happens to the twig when the weather changes. Mark the right spots (see drawing 5), and then bring the hygrometer inside to finish it. You can get some ideas from the color photograph.

COZY COTTAGE

This charming shingled cottage is especially nice because of its heavy brown roof made of pine cone scales.

THE COTTAGE

MATERIALS

- some pieces of yellow wood veneer that you either buy at a crafts or hobby shop, or make from a small wooden box (such as a cigar box) and paint yellow with very diluted gouache paints
- burnt wooden matchsticks
- black and beige construction paper or Bristol board
- some nice pine cone scales that match; you need some narrower ones for the top of the roof—take them from the tip of a pine cone
- white glue, pen-knife, ruler

CONSTRUCTION

The Cottage Walls

- Draw the outline of the cottage on beige construction paper following drawing 1.
- With a pen-knife and ruler, go over all the fold lines (the broken lines), but do not fold.
- For the balcony, draw a line about $\frac{3}{4}$ inch (2 cm.) from the bottom (line A in drawing 2) and another one about $\frac{1}{4}$ inch (1 cm.) higher (line B in drawing 2).
- Cut the wooden veneer into "shingles" about 1 inch × $\frac{3}{8}$ inch (25 mm. × 9 mm.).
- Draw doors and windows on the construction paper.

- Glue the shingles in straight lines, following drawing 3. Cover all the sides of the cottage. Be sure to: re-cut the shingles so you don't cover the doors and windows; cut the shingles at the edges of the fold lines on the sides; glue the shingles over the fold lines for the peaks of the roof. When the glue is dry, re-fold the glueing tabs (see drawing 1) and re-cut the shingles as shown in drawing 4.
- Fold and glue together the sides of the cottage.

glueing tabs for the roof

shingle

group of shingles

where top and front meet

16

The Balcony

● Paint 25 to 30 burnt wooden matchsticks with brown gouache paint. Varnish them and let them dry.

● Glue the matchsticks between lines A and B as shown in drawing 5.

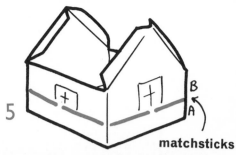

5

matchsticks

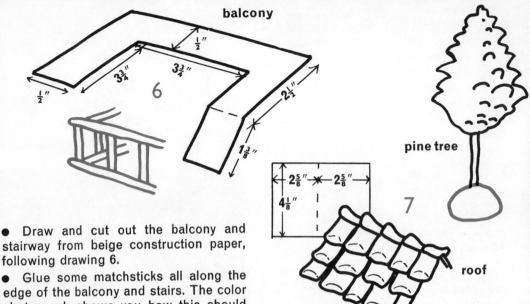

balcony

$\frac{1}{2}''$

$3\frac{3}{4}''$ $3\frac{3}{4}''$

$\frac{1}{2}''$

6

$2\frac{1}{2}''$

$1\frac{3}{8}''$

pine tree

$2\frac{5}{8}''$ — $2\frac{5}{8}''$

$4\frac{1}{8}''$

7

roof

● Draw and cut out the balcony and stairway from beige construction paper, following drawing 6.

● Glue some matchsticks all along the edge of the balcony and stairs. The color photograph shows you how this should look.

● Cut about 30 pieces about $\frac{1}{4}$ inch (1 cm.) long from some matchsticks to make the bars.

● Glue these pieces to the matchsticks edging the balcony. Cut the ends of the matches on a slant for the stairs (see the color photograph).

● Now you have to make the handrail for the balcony and the stairs. Glue matchsticks end to end to fit along the stairway and the balcony. Put some glue on the ends of each match bar and then place these matchsticks on top of them. Varnish the matchsticks again. Then add some more glue under the matches on line A.

The Roof

● Cut a piece of black construction paper following drawing 7.

● Go over the broken fold line at the middle with a pen-knife (do not cut through the paper).

● On each side of the roof, glue on 3 lines of scales, overlapping the rows as shown in drawing 7. Carefully fold the roof in half on the fold line.

● Glue on the small scales to make the peak of the roof (see drawing 7).

● Fold the glue tabs on the body of the cottage. Put some glue on them and place the roof right on.

THE PINE TREES

MATERIALS

For each tree you need:

● a medium-sized pine cone
● a twig for the trunk
● a small ball of modelling clay

CONSTRUCTION

● Cut a piece of twig as long as you want for the trunk.

● With green gouache, paint the tips of the pine cone's scales.

● Make a ball of modelling clay. Push the end of the trunk into the clay. Then put some glue on the other end of the trunk and stick the tree on it.

● Let the tree dry well. Shape the clay so the little tree stands up straight.

berry wall hanging

This decorative panel is easy to make. All you use are some pine needles, some pine cones and some red beads (you can just as easily use some hazel nuts) to make this pretty hanging.

MATERIALS

- a piece of stiff cardboard
- some cloth ¾ inch (4 cm.) larger on all sides than the cardboard
- some pine cones and pretty pine needles
- red beads or hazelnuts
- glue, varnish
- a picture hanger

CONSTRUCTION

- Clean and varnish the pine cones. Let them dry.
- Spread some white glue on the cardboard. Turn the cardboard over. Place it right in the middle of the piece of cloth (see drawing 1). Fold over the edges of the cloth in back and glue them to the cardboard (drawing 2 shows how to do this). Make the corners very straight. You can glue a piece of cardboard under the panel to make it very neat.
- Arrange the pine needles, pine cones and beads in the prettiest way you can.
- Use a few drops of glue to hold the parts in place. Put the "hearts" of the pine cones (see drawing 3) in different directions.
- Glue a picture hanger on the back of the panel.

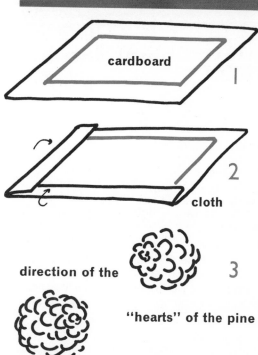

cardboard

cloth

direction of the

"hearts" of the pine

Christmas decorations

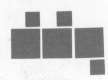

Here are three original ideas for decorating a Christmas table or Christmas tree. Of course, you can use the candle or the star at other times, too.

LITTLE CHRISTMAS TREES

You can easily make different types of decorative little Christmas trees.

MATERIALS

● a large pine cone
● something for a base; here, a cube of cork was used, but you can use a piece of wood, a large bottle cork, or even modelling clay
● some small beads, plastic stars, or some plastic "jewels"; to make the decorations shinier, glue a little piece of aluminum foil or silver paper to the back
● some small birthday candles; if they seem too big, cut them with a knife
● some tinsel or, as shown in the color photograph, a string of tiny silver beads
● green gouache paint, glue

CONSTRUCTION

● Paint the ends of the pine cone's scales with green gouache. Let it dry.
● Glue the tree to its base, using the same method you learned on page 18.
● Carefully arrange the string of beads on the "tree."
● Decorate the tree by glueing on the rest of the ornaments. Let everything dry.

cube of cork

A CHRISTMAS STAR

Here is a very bright Christmas decoration to put on a wall or to hang from a ceiling or light. Be careful if you hang the star, because it is heavy (don't forget that pine cones are wooden!). You must use strong string.

MATERIALS

● 6 same-sized pine cones which look as much alike as possible
● cardboard, gold-colored paper
● thick, strong string
● a brightly colored Christmas ball about 1¾ inches (4 cm.) in diameter
● 6 large wooden beads
● gold paint in a tube (any brand is fine)
● scissors, pen-knife, large needle, glue, ruler

CONSTRUCTION

- On the cardboard, draw a strip $1\frac{1}{4}$ inches (3 cm.) wide × 12 inches (29 cm.) long. Starting at one end, draw some lines across the width every $1\frac{7}{8}$ inches (4.5 cm.). A small piece $\frac{3}{4}$ inch (2 cm.) long is left at the end. You will use it as a glueing tab.

- Cut out the strip. Draw over the lines with the pen-knife to help you fold the cardboard.

- Cut the gold paper following drawing 1.

- Carefully fold the cardboard along the lines you "drew" with the knife (see drawing 2). Glue the gold paper to the inside part marked A in drawing 1. Then shape the cardboard hexagon by glueing the tab at the top (see drawing 3).

- Glue the tabs of the gold paper marked B and then the tabs marked C (see drawings 3 and 4).

- Attach a piece of string to the Christmas ball by the hook on the ball. Tie a very large, strong knot about $\frac{1}{4}$ inch (1 cm.) above the ball.

- Thread the string into the large needle. Sew right through the middle of one of the corners of the cardboard (see drawing 5).

- Glue the pine cones on each side of the hexagon. To make sure the glue will hold, put some glue on the base of the cone and the part of the cardboard it touches. Let the glue dry a little and then put on another drop of glue. Put the pine cone in place.

- Glue a wooden bead between each pine cone. If you aren't going to hang this ornament from a ceiling or light, make a large knot on the string at the corner. Put on a drop of glue along about $\frac{1}{4}$ inch (1 cm.) of the string to hold the knot.

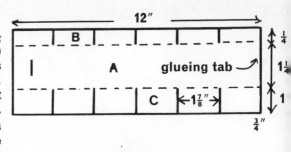

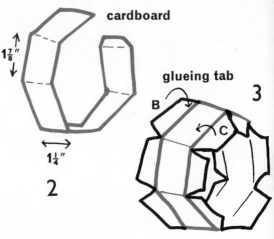

cardboard

glueing tab

3

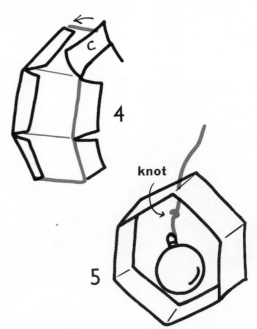

2

4

5

knot

A CANDLE HOLDER

MATERIALS

a large red candle

5 medium-sized pine cones which look as much alike as possible

10 scales from a very dry pine cone, the same size as the other 5

a thin nail

cardboard

red and green gouache paint, varnish

about 30 gold beads

glue, thread, needle

nippers or wire cutters

CONSTRUCTION

● With nippers or wire cutters, cut the 5 pine cones in half. Remove the middle fibres; you will be left with a kind of flower (see drawing 1).

● Paint the top pine cone scales with bright red gouache paint. When the paint is dry, varnish the flower.

● String the gold beads on a thread as shown in drawing 2. Place 5 beads around the one in the middle. Make 5 of these groups.

● Glue one gold bead group into the middle of each flower.

● Paint the 10 loose pine cone scales green and then varnish them.

● From cardboard, cut a circle 4 inches (10 cm.) in diameter. Paint it with green gouache.

● Push the nail through the cardboard right in the middle of the circle. The point of the nail should face upwards.

● Put some glue on the base of the candle. Then push the candle into the nail (see drawing 3).

● Glue the flowers all around the candle (see drawing 4).

● Between each flower, glue two scales.

This candle holder is mostly decorative. If you want to light the candle, remember that the pine cones on the bottom will burn easily, so you must be sure to watch it carefully.

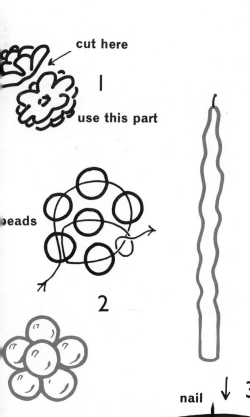

cut here

use this part

beads

2

nail ↓ 3

4

Lamp
and SHADE

This pretty and original lamp is decorated with pine cone scales. And it is not hard to make at all!

Choose one large pine cone and at least 2 medium-sized ones. These pine cones should be old enough so that you can easily remove the scales. Pick very dry pine cones that are still reddish brown, and not black.

If a scale is hard to take off, hold it firmly in the middle between your thumb and index finger. Move the scale carefully back and forth, from side to side. When the scale comes out, clean its base by scraping off any rough material or resin on it.

MATERIALS

● some pine cones; for the "rose" on the shade, the scales must all come from the same pine cone
● a lamp shade about 12 inches (30 cm.) in diameter
● a nicely shaped bottle
● glue
● a lamp-wiring kit to put in the neck of the bottle
● paper
● crayon or soft-tipped marker
● varnish, fine brush for spreading it

CONSTRUCTION

Lamp Base

● Clean the bottle.
● Sort the scales, choosing the nices[t] widest and longest (those from th[e] middle of the cone).
● Glue the scales in rows onto the bott[le] at the bottom and overlap the rows (se[e] drawing 1). For easy glueing, spread glu[e] on the back of 5 or 6 scales and let th[e] glue dry a moment while you put glue o[n] 5 or 6 more scales. Then put the scales i[n] place, adding more glue if necessary.
● Continue to the place where the bott[le] narrows to form the neck. End with a ro[w] of small scales glued as shown i[n] drawing 2.
● After the glue is dry, if you can see th[e] bottle through the scales in some spot[s] glue some smaller scales underneath.
● Varnish the base and let it dry.

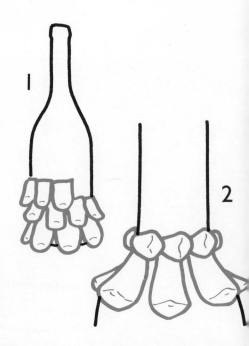

Lamp Shade

● Begin by taking the smallest scales from the end of a pine cone (see drawing 3). Arrange 7 or 8 of them in a row in front of you, smallest ones first, larger ones following. Do not use any broken scales.

● Draw a snail shape, like the one shown in the color photograph, on paper with a crayon or soft-tipped marker. Place the piece of paper inside the shade (if necessary, attach the paper to the edge of the shade with large paper clips). You can see the design through the shade (see drawing 4).

● Glue the scales on the shade, following the color photograph. Start with the smallest scales in the middle.

● After you have glued all the scales in place, varnish them with a fine brush. Try not to get any varnish on the shade itself.

● Now make the "braids" on the top and bottom of the lamp shade. Glue on some medium-sized, same-shaped (if possible) scales one after the other. Overlap these scales as shown in drawing 5.

● Varnish the braids with a fine brush.

FINISHING

● Put the lamp-wiring kit into the bottle. Add the shade and a light bulb.

Wait until the lamp and shade are completely dry before lighting the lamp. At first, don't leave the lamp on too long, or the heat will ruin the glued parts. Later on, when the glue is better set, the heat from the bulb will not hurt it.

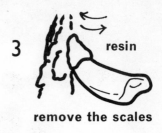

3   resin

remove the scales

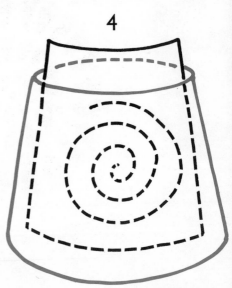

4

design as seen through shade

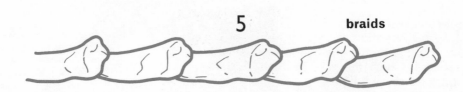

5   braids

flowers

You can make beautiful flowers using pine cones and all kinds of other materials. Then, you can make some very pretty bouquets.

The middle of the flowers shown here were made from cones of the larch tree, but you can use any pine cones you can find for your creations.

MATERIALS

pine cones

large and small burnt wooden matches, wooden toothpicks, brightly colored beads and dried pumpkin seeds (or any other similar decorative materials)

wood shavings or pieces of veneer, both natural and colored

gouache paints, varnish

stiff wire for the stems

wood glue, green florists' tape for the stems

a pick or other sharp tool

CONSTRUCTION

The Red Flower

You make all the flowers in the same way. You will find it is easier if you glue the pine cones to the stems first.

With the pick, make a small hole in the woody base of the pine cone. Push the wire in about $\frac{1}{2}$ inch (8–10 mm.). Pull the wire out again. Then put a drop of glue into the hole and onto the end of the wire (see drawing 1). Push the wire in again and let it dry for about 2 hours.

● Take some red wood shavings or pieces of veneer. To make the petals flat, "curl" the wood carefully in the direction of the grain with the back of a scissors blade.

● Cut out 5 petals following the shape in drawing 2. Make the petals the right size for the pine cone middle.

● Put some glue on the bottom of each petal. Let them dry a little. Then put the petals in place (see drawing 3).

● Stick in the little matches as shown in drawing 3.

● Varnish the matches and the cone, but not the wood shavings.

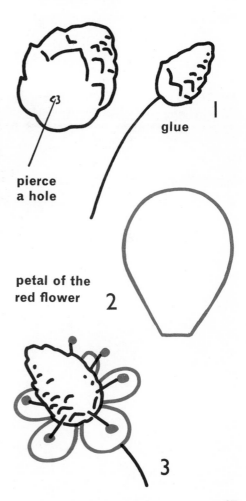

pierce a hole

glue

1

petal of the red flower

2

3

27

The Green Flower

Make the green flower the same as the red one, using 6 petals you make following drawing 4) from green shavings.

● Varnish the flower.

● Put on the beads (see drawing 5).

The Tulip

Here you use the shavings with their natural curl to make curved tulip petals (see drawing 6).

● First put 5 pumpkin seeds onto the pine cone (see drawing 7). Carefully paint them with bright yellow gouache. Then varnish them.

● Then glue on the petals the same way you glued the petals for the red flower above.

4

green flower

5

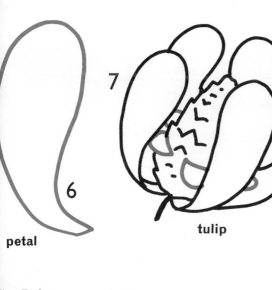

7

6

petal

tulip

8

daisy

The Daisy

You will use toothpicks for this spiky blossom.

● Varnish the pine cone.

● Cut the toothpicks if you think they are too long to make a daisy like the one in the color photograph. Glue the toothpicks in place on the pine cone. Use as many as you want, to make a pretty "wheel," as shown in drawing 8. Let the glue dry.

● Place a thin line of glue on the other end of each toothpick. Let the glue dry a little. Then put on a pumpkin seed.

● When the glue is dry, varnish the seeds.

The Brown Flower

● Take 10 pretty scales from a pine cone.

● Put glue on their bottoms. Arrange the scales in 2 circles between the scales of a small pine cone. Overlap the scales as shown in drawing 10.

● Glue a small match between each scale in the top row and under the scales of the bottom row (see drawing 9).

● Varnish the flower.

● To finish this flower, glue 5 rose-colored beads to the petals in the top row.

Of course, you can go on to make lots of other beautiful flowers, like those below!

9 | brown flower

front view

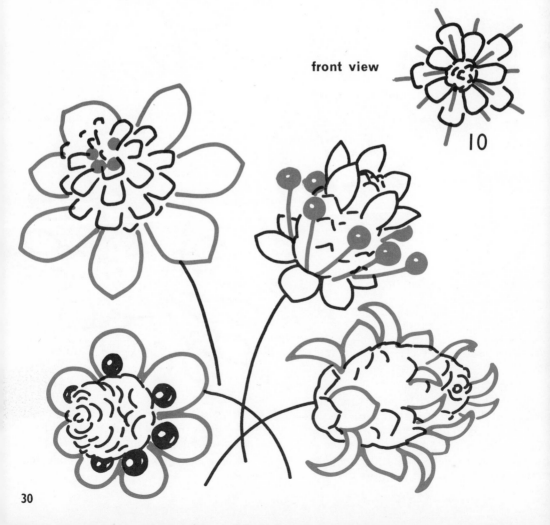

10

30

a small
GARDEN

Here is a small garden that you can play with for a long time. You can make it the garden of your dreams just by placing the rocks and flowering bushes wherever you want. You can move them in lots of different ways to make many different gardens.

You can also use these same natural "playthings" to decorate a model train track very inexpensively!

MATERIALS

● various sizes and shapes of pine cones

● gouache paints in different shades of green and other bright colors for the flowers

● modelling clay that you can paint after it dries

● lids and tops from jars for flower pots

● some pebbles and sand

● a large piece of cardboard (or a sheet of plywood) for a base; cover the base with green construction paper, felt or some other type of green textured paper or cloth

● a small mirror for the pond

● glue, varnish

CONSTRUCTION

● Make the different things for your garden in any order you want. You are the "gardener," so you decide what to do first!

● Color the tips of the pine cones' scales for the flowering bushes with some gouache paint.

● Then paint the trees with different shades of green.

● Glue some of the flowering bushes into the "pots." Put others on lumps of modelling clay which you can flatten to hold them still.

● Simply place the pine cone trees on their bottoms. But, you can also make trunks for them (see the trees for the cottage on page 18).

● You can create very different effects by varnishing only some of the painted trees and bushes.

● To arrange your garden, put the trees, flowers and sand for the walks, the mirror for the water and the pebbles (which you can varnish if you want) wherever you want. The fun of this toy is that you can easily change your garden as many times as you want!

 **INDEX**